# Dorothea Lange

By Susan Martins Miller

Wright Group

The McGraw-Hill Companies

# www.WrightGroup.com

 **Wright Group**

# Contents

# Historical Time Line

Dorothea Lange lived through a very dramatic time in American history. The Great Depression devastated the American economy. The wind storms that whipped through the Southwest destroyed farmland and homes. Japanese planes attacked the United States, forcing the nation to enter World War II. The time line below shows important moments in Dorothea Lange's life and significant events that happened in the world around her.

The stock market crashes and the Great Depression begins.

World War I ends.

Dorothea Lange is born in Hoboken, New Jersey.

Dorothea gets her first job in a photography studio.

Dorothea moves to California.

**1895**  **1913**  **1918**  **1929**

**1902**  **1914**  **1919**  **1930**

Dorothea contracts polio.

Dorothea Lange marries Maynard Dixon.

World War I begins.

Astronomers discover the planet Pluto.

Japanese planes attack Pearl Harbor and the United States enters World War II.

Disney releases *Snow White*.

Adolf Hitler becomes chancellor of Germany.

The first blood bank opens in Chicago.

The first color television set is invented.

Dorothea Lange dies of cancer at age 70.

**1932**   **1933**   **1935**   **1937**   **1939**   **1941**   **1945**   **1946**   **1957**   **1965**

Dorothea marries Paul Taylor.

Franklin Delano Roosevelt is elected president.

Elvis Presley is born.

World War II begins.

The United States drops atomic bombs on Japan to end World War II.

Dr. Seuss writes *The Cat in the Hat*.

# Author's Note

What do you see when you look at one of Dorothea Lange's photographs? I see real people with real emotions. I feel their struggles, their heartaches, and their joys. I wonder what their lives were really like.

Dorothea Lange used her pictures to tell the stories of thousands of people. Most people do not know how difficult her own story was. She loved her sons and wanted to be a good mother. At times, she set her work aside to focus on her family. However, she was not very happy during these times. Her work called her to use her gifts, and she answered the call over and over again. Her sons often paid the price of her gift with their own unhappiness.

In spite of this, Dorothea Lange was an amazing American who found courage in thousands of other Americans she thought were amazing. And because of her, their courage inspires us as well.

*Susan Martins Miller*

# "I'd Like to Take Your Picture"

On a rainy April afternoon in 1935, a woman with a camera pulled into a California gas station. She had been driving a long time and got out of the car to stretch her legs. Across the parking lot, she saw a car full of people who looked sad and lost. The license plate told her that they were from Oklahoma. Her photographer's eye was drawn to them.

*In this photo, Dorothea Lange captures the journey of a traveling family in California*

She walked over to them and asked if they were looking for work. "We've been blown out," they told her. Ferocious dust storms had twisted through Oklahoma, they explained. Wind had destroyed their farm. There were no other jobs in Oklahoma, so they packed up the car and headed to California. They hoped they could become **migrant workers**.

Dorothea paid for her gas and pulled her car back out onto the highway. But the discouraged faces of the Oklahoma family haunted her. They must have been desperate. What else would make them leave everything behind to go to a new state so far away?

*States ravaged by dust storms depended heavily on farming. The shaded portions of the map show the area that became known as the Dust Bowl.*

Dorothea kept driving. She was astonished when she saw another family from Oklahoma pulled over to the side of the road, and then another and another. For several hundred

*Dorothea took this picture of two men walking toward Los Angeles*

miles, Dorothea saw families that had come from far away. They were all stranded along the California highway.

On the trip home, Dorothea stopped to talk to dozens of people along the road. They were all victims of the dust storms in Oklahoma. As she took their pictures and listened to their

stories, Dorothea realized that she was witnessing history. This was the beginning of the great **migration** of farm families to the Western states. She would remember this day for the rest of her life.

*This photo by Dorothea Lange shows the hopelessness of many of the families who chose to move west in the 1930s*

# Leap Back in Time

Daily life and clothing have evolved tremendously since Dorothea Lange's lifetime. Look at the objects on these pages. We still use many of them today, only in a more advanced form. For example, most of us use CD players or MP3 players to listen to music instead of records or jukeboxes. The phones in our houses have buttons, not dials. Most are even cordless. However, some toys and other forms of entertainment from the 30s and 40s are still around in their original form, like the yo-yo.

YO-YO

FAMILY GATHERING
AROUND RADIO, 193

TELEPHONE

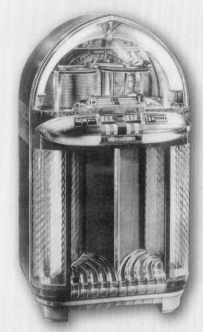

JUKEBOX

TRANSISTOR
RADIO

BENNY
GOODMAN

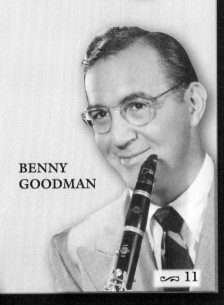

# CHAPTER TWO

# Teacher or Photographer?

**H**enry and Joan Nutzholm lived in Hoboken, New Jersey when their daughter, Dorothea, was born on May 26, 1895. Six years later a boy, Martin, was born into the family. Henry worked as a lawyer. Joan sang in local concerts and cared for the children.

*Dorothea's childhood home is shown in this photo*

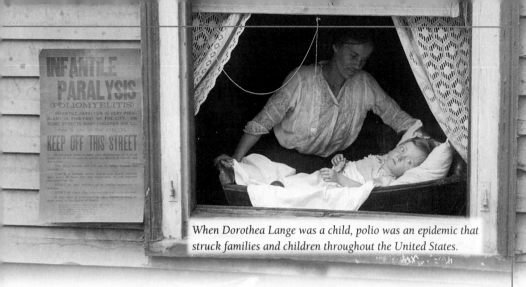

When Dorothea Lange was a child, polio was an epidemic that struck families and children throughout the United States.

Hard times for the family began when Dorothea was struck by polio at the age of seven. At that time, there was no way to prevent polio and no way to cure it. Dorothea had a high fever for many days. Her head, back, and legs hurt. When the fever was gone, her right leg was damaged. Children laughed at her and called her "Limpy." Her mother used to tell her to "walk as well as you can," but this did not make Dorothea feel any better.

## In Their Own Words

"It was perhaps the most important thing that happened to me. It formed me, guided me, instructed me, helped me, and humiliated me."

~Dorothea Lange about having polio

*Workers still travel daily by ferry from Hoboken to New York, but many people now take the train.*

When Dorothea was 12, her father left the family. He never sent them any money. Joan decided to change her last name back to Lange, her name before she married Dorothea's father. Dorothea also took Lange as her last name.

The family could not afford to live in their comfortable house, so they moved in with Dorothea's grandmother. Joan got a job at the New York Public Library. Every day, Dorothea and her mother rode the ferry from Hoboken, New Jersey to New York City. Dorothea went to school in New York. After school, she went to the library to wait for her mother. She was supposed to do her homework, but usually she didn't.

*Did You Know...* President Franklin Delano Roosevelt is another famous person who had polio. Jonas Salk discovered a vaccine for polio, and vaccinations began in 1955. Children who are not immunized can still get the disease today.

Dorothea never liked school and was not a good student. She preferred to visit the museums and art shows of New York, soaking up the sights and sounds of the city.

When Dorothea was almost finished with high school, her mother began to worry. How was Dorothea going to support herself? Joan thought Dorothea should become a teacher. But at 17, Dorothea declared that she wanted to be a photographer. She had never even owned a camera. She did not know anything about photography. Her mother thought the idea was ridiculous and insisted that Dorothea go to college.

*In 1929, Dorothea Lange used a twin lens Rolleiflex camera.*

*The Metropolitan Museum of Art in New York City may have been one of the museums Dorothea Lange visited for inspiration.*

Dorothea did not like college any more than she had liked high school. She got a job in a photography studio where she took orders and learned how to frame photographs. Although her mother was not happy about it, Dorothea dropped out of college, determined to become a photographer.

Arnold Genthe, a successful photographer, gave Dorothea her first job in a photography studio. Later, he gave her a camera and taught her how to use it.

## In Their Own Words

**"I decided, almost on a certain day, that I was going to be a photographer."**

~Dorothea Lange, photojournalist

# CHAPTER THREE

# On Her Own

**W**hen Dorothea Lange was 23 years old, she was ready to see the world. Her best friend was ready for an adventure, too. Together they had $140, and with that they set out on their journey.

They traveled to Louisiana, New Mexico, and San Francisco, California. In San Francisco, a pickpocket stole all of their money, forcing them to stay and find work. Because of her experience working for a photographer, Dorothea found a job right away. She worked developing pictures and noticed that some of the photographs were very interesting. This made her want to be a photographer even more. She started taking photographs of her own.

*Dorothea and her friend, Florence, arrived in San Francisco five months after leaving Hoboken. Dorothea lived the rest of her life in California.*

Before long, someone offered to help Dorothea set up her own photography studio. She quickly became recognized as one of the best photographers in San Francisco. Many people who wanted her to take their pictures were wealthy, so her business did very well.

*Dorothea Lange took this image of a poor child in Arizona.*

Two years after arriving in San Francisco, Dorothea married Maynard Dixon, a painter. Dorothea traveled with Maynard to Arizona, where he painted scenes on a Native American **reservation**. For the first time, Dorothea saw the poverty of many of the children, the crowded schools, and the sense of hopelessness of many of the Native American people who lived there. While Maynard was busy sketching and painting, Dorothea photographed the world around her.

*Dorothea's husband painting in Arizona*

Maynard was away a lot because of his painting. After they had children, Dorothea cared for the two boys on her own. Because she wanted to keep up with her photography, she made the hard decision to send her boys to live with other families for weeks at a time, or to boarding school.

*Dorothea and Maynard visited their boys on the weekends at boarding school.*

As Dorothea's reputation as a photographer grew, the United States was plunged into a state of turmoil. On October 24, 1929, the **stock market** crashed, and the value of stocks suddenly dropped to almost nothing. People who had invested their savings in the stock market now had no money. Banks and businesses around the country began to close. Very quickly, a lot of people were out of work. The **Great Depression** had begun.

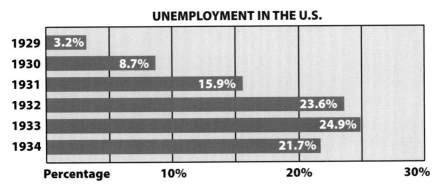

**UNEMPLOYMENT IN THE U.S.**

| Year | Percentage |
|------|-----------|
| 1929 | 3.2% |
| 1930 | 8.7% |
| 1931 | 15.9% |
| 1932 | 23.6% |
| 1933 | 24.9% |
| 1934 | 21.7% |

Percentage    10%    20%    30%

*This chart shows the sharp rise of unemployment during the Great Depression.*

*Dorothea Lange looked for the best angles for her photographs. She used a camera that she held at her waist and looked down into it.*

One day, Dorothea looked out her window to the street below. She felt drawn to take a camera and go down to the street to photograph people there. Dorothea photographed the White Angel bread line. A woman called the "White Angel" set up a **soup kitchen**. All different kinds of people came for free meals. All of them were poor. As she took pictures outside of her studio, she realized that her most important work was not making portraits of wealthy clients.

*With the photograph* White Angel Bread Line, San Francisco, 1933, *Dorothea began to use her pictures to help struggling people.*

# CHAPTER FOUR

# The Story of a Nation

**W**hen she first heard of drought and dust storms in Oklahoma, Dorothea did not know they would change her life. Thousands of families left their farms and moved to California, where Dorothea lived. They were desperate to find a new life. Instead, they found only hopelessness.

When Dorothea Lange had her first photography exhibit in 1934, a professor named Paul Taylor at the University of California came to see it. He recognized Dorothea's talent right away. Paul was studying the effects of the Great Depression for the government, and he invited Dorothea to help. She would take the pictures. He would write the words.

*Dust storms made the sky black in the middle of the day and carried tons of soil off empty farm fields.*

While Dorothea's professional life flourished, her personal life was falling apart. She and Maynard had not been happy together for a long time. In 1935, Dorothea divorced Maynard and married Paul Taylor.

*Dorothea and Paul*

They were together for the rest of Dorothea's life.

Together, Paul and Dorothea visited places where migrant workers were stuck with no work and no place to go. Whenever they went somewhere new, they began a conversation with the people they met. Dorothea always asked permission before she took someone's picture. She wanted people to know that she was trying to help by sending pictures to the government.

*Dorothea married Paul because she wanted to share her life with someone who felt as strongly as she did about improving people's lives.*

# Counterpoint

Dorothea Lange felt strongly about helping migrant workers have better conditions and fair pay. Some farm owners felt differently. Because so many people were looking for work, they could pay very little. Some orchard owners took advantage of their workers by paying as little as one dollar for picking an entire ton of peaches. This attitude made Dorothea very angry. She was trying to help those in need. Opposition from farm owners did not help the cause.

Dorothea's work now was very different from what she was used to. She once said, "I didn't know a mule from a tractor when I started." But she did not let her inexperience stop her. She took some of her most famous pictures during these years, including *Migrant Mother*.

This picture almost never happened. One day, Dorothea drove past a sign that she could not get out of her mind. The sign led her to a woman from Oklahoma and her children in a pea field.

Their pea crop had frozen, so it could not be harvested. The family ate the frozen peas and the birds that the children killed with stones. Just before Dorothea arrived, the mother had sold the tires off her car for money to buy food.

Dorothea asked if she could take the woman's picture. Somehow, the woman knew that Dorothea was trying to help. The picture would let other people know how serious the problems facing migrant workers were. Dorothea wanted to make sure the government found a way to help the migrant mother and the many others like her.

One of Lange's most famous pictures is *Migrant Mother, Nipomo, California, 1936.* Notice the children hiding their faces. How do you think they felt?

Dorothea did not try to cheer people up with her pictures. Instead, her photographs documented what was happening in the United States. In this way, Dorothea became one of the first **photojournalists**.

Dorothea's career was going very well. Her home life, however, continued to be difficult. She loved her sons very much and tried to be a good mother, but she felt guilty about sending her boys to live with other people so she could work. Sometimes, the stress made her feel sick. She began to have frequent pains in her stomach.

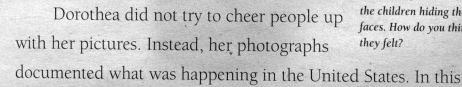

**Did You Know...** While people like Dorothea Lange made a photographic record of migrant workers, authors like John Steinbeck wrote novels to tell the same story. His most famous book is *The Grapes of Wrath*, published in 1939. It tells the story of a family from Oklahoma who moved to California.

# CHAPTER FIVE

# Pictures Worth Ten Thousand Words

*I*n 1941, Dorothea won a Guggenheim Fellowship. This allowed her to take a year to photograph whatever she chose. She decided to take pictures of some unique religious groups in the United States: the Hutterites of South Dakota, the Amana Society in Iowa, and the Mormons in Utah.

But far away from these peaceful societies, trouble lurked around the world. Adolf Hitler and the **Nazi** party rose to power in Germany, striking terror across Europe. On December 7, 1941, the Japanese attacked the U.S. naval port at Pearl Harbor, Hawaii. Consequently, the United States entered World War II.

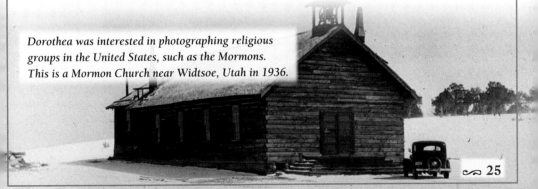

*Dorothea was interested in photographing religious groups in the United States, such as the Mormons. This is a Mormon Church near Widtsoe, Utah in 1936.*

In her photo Mochida Family Awaiting Evacuation Bus, 1942, *Dorothea* shows how evacuation tags were used to keep families together while they moved to internment camps.

Japanese families had been in the United States for several generations, but after Japan attacked the United States, many Americans became suspicious of people of Japanese heritage. President Franklin Delano Roosevelt even signed an order that forced over 120,000 people of Japanese descent to leave their homes and move to **internment** camps.

*Did You Know...* Before the Japanese attack on Pearl Harbor, many Americans thought that the war did not have anything to do with them.

The Office of War Information hired Dorothea to document the internment. Even though this was her job, she did not believe it was fair to treat Japanese Americans this way. They

*Dorothea (top right) photographs Japanese Americans being sent to internment camps in this 1942 photo.*

were citizens, and they had not broken any laws. Yet they were being sent to a prison. The real reason was racial prejudice.

Dorothea was horrified. If the government could take away the rights of one group of citizens, maybe they would do the same thing to other people. Some days, it was very hard for her to take the pictures. But she took them so she could tell the true story of the Japanese Americans.

## Making Amends

In 1942, because of the Japanese attack on Pearl Harbor, most Americans believed that moving Japanese Americans to internment camps was the right thing to do. In January of 1945, however, the government closed the camps, and the Japanese Americans were allowed to go home. In 1988, President Ronald Reagan signed a law apologizing for the internment and providing $20,000 to each person who had been in one of the camps.

Terrified Horse *from Dorothea Lange's famous project* Death of a Valley

About this time, Dorothea became seriously ill. She had an operation to remove a large part of her stomach. As she recovered, she looked for a new focus for her work.

In the years that followed, Dorothea worked on many different projects. In 1945, the government asked her to photograph a conference in San Francisco. This conference established the United Nations.

Dorothea also did several assignments for *Life* magazine, which was well-known for the quality of the pictures it published. Her most famous project was *Death of a Valley*, published in *Aperture* magazine. This series of photographs showed how desperately people living in northern California needed a major water supply.

**Did You Know...** *Life* magazine was first published in 1936. It is still famous for the extraordinary photographs it uses to tell stories about real life.

In the 1950s and 1960s, Dorothea traveled with her husband to work on projects in other parts of the world. She and Paul went to Asia, Egypt, the Near East, and Ecuador in South America. She took pictures everywhere she went. Unfortunately, her stomach continued to bother her, and she began to stay closer to home.

Family on Street Corner, Ecuador, 1960

In August of 1964, Dorothea was diagnosed with cancer of the esophagus. No operation could help her, so she prepared to die. Her final photography project was of her family. Dorothea loved taking pictures of her grandchildren and the family's beach cottage. She called this series of family photos *To a Cabin*.

Dorothea received one final honor before she died. The Museum of Modern Art in New York planned a major show of her life's work. From tens of thousands of negatives, Dorothea chose 200 pictures for the exhibit.

Dorothea Lange died from cancer on October 11, 1965. The show to honor her was held three months later.

*Dorothea's photo* Helen and Andrew, 1955, *is of the son of Dorothea's son, John.*

# Conclusion

As a child, Dorothea Lange's eyes absorbed life around her, the good and the bad. As a teenager, she discovered that she could use a camera to show other people what she saw through her eyes. She used this gift to speak out against injustice and to reveal beauty. Dorothea Lange reminded a nation of the courage and dignity of its citizens.

*Dorothea Lange prepares to take another photo*

# Glossary

**Great Depression** in the United States, a period of severe economic hardship beginning in 1929 and continuing throughout the 1930s

**internment** living within boundaries; confined

**migrant workers** workers who travel from farm to farm looking for employment

**migration** movement of large groups from one place to another

**Nazi** during World War II, a follower of German leader Adolf Hitler, who believed in strict government control of everything in the country

**photojournalists** people who report the news and other factual information through photographs

**reservation** land set apart by the government for Native Americans to use

**soup kitchen** a place where people in need can get a free meal

**stock market** the place where stocks (portions of a company or business that people are able to buy) are bought and sold

# Index